Author
James Benedict Is a teacher, writer, and storyteller. His stories show goodness can come in hopeless situations. James teaches, and inspires people of all ages. He has taught in top Universities in Taiwan and Japan .

Acknowledgment
I thank God who inspires me to write. Thanks to my lovely wife and my supportive family. Also thanks to my amazing children and students to whom I have told stories, for many years.
- James Benedict

Disclaimer

First printing edition 2025.
Publisher: James Benedict
Language : English
Paperback
Dimensions : 6 x 9 inches

The tale of a leader, against all odds,
Faced tough battles, Without breaking laws.

Despite the noise, the doubts, the fight,
He returned, his presence so bright.

His rallies loud, his words so bold,
He won hearts in ways untold.

With every fight, he stayed strong,
People protested, but he grew his
throne

Other leaders with hopes to lead,
joined the cause, a shift to see,
Many names, many voices of pride,
Stood against, also changed sides.

.

Another women, sharp and clear,
Called out opposition for what she'd fear.
"You jailed for pot, and smoked your share,"
A debate moment, fiery and rare.

Podcasts and voices, reach so wide,
Brought new support to leader's side.

Rich and Powerful, with money and might,
Helped him soar into the night.

Boxer danced, a champ on fire,
Everyone shout his name and inspire.

Then he drove a truck through crowds so steep,
To show the world, "No job is cheap."

He served burgers with a red cap,
Saying, "Hard work builds the map."

He served ice cream, apron black,
In a truck on the streets, no pride to lack.

Scandals, trials, yet he stood tall,
A surprise victory stunned them all.

Many attempts on his life were dared,
Yet he survived with people's prayer.

Each player a piece in the grand game's art,
Yet he emerged, a force apart.

Against them all, he made his stand,
Claiming again the leader's brand.

Through twists and turns, he stayed true,
Promising change, a future new.